Honoured

Acknowledgements
Many thanks to the following who have published or broadcast some of these poems: And Other Poems website (andotherpoems. wordpress.com), *Brittle Star*, Buxton Poetry Competition, Campaign To Free Gilad Shalit, *Cardinal Points*, Gold Dust Magazine (youtube.com/watch?v=1xuA9sCCaz8), *Ha'aretz*, Ha'aretz.com, *Jerusalem Post, Jewish Quarterly, Jewish Renaissance, Joker Magazine*, JW3 (youtube.com/watch?v=9UVkhAjlu_8), londongrip.co.uk, *PN Review, Poems In The Waiting Room*, Poetry Please BBC Radio 4.

Honoured

Yvonne Green

smith|doorstop

Published 2015 by
smith|doorstop Books
The Poetry Business
Bank Street Arts
32-40 Bank Street
Sheffield S1 2DS
www.poetrybusiness.co.uk

Copyright © Yvonne Green 2015

ISBN 978-1-910367-56-8

British Library Cataloguing-in-Publication Data.
A catalogue record for this book is available from the
British Library.

Designed and typeset by Utter
Printed by Printondemand.com
Cover image: Seder © Nicole Eisenman
Collection The Jewish Museum, New York
Courtesy the artist
Author photo: Brian Green

smith|doorstop is a member of Inpress,
www.inpressbooks.co.uk. Distributed by Central Books Ltd.,
99 Wallis Road, London E9 5LN.

The Poetry Business is an Arts Council
National Portfolio Organisation

Contents

Honoured

Jews

For Kayla and Lilia

This Is Not Your History

An End

Charcoal from her pencils
smoulders in the *brascenos*,
where, long ago, boards
replaced windows,
and fathers sealed front doors

while mothers sewed up leg-slits
in hearth-blankets,
then bibbed their children
face-to-the-fumes.

This Is Not Your History

You surrender to my music,
story, food, unconsciously.
Forget your own. Afraid
it will control you.

We make war and love,
differently to you.
Pepper, salt, and hyssop,
change things and God
has many names.

Not-God, many explanations.
A slice mimed above the head,
across the throat. An eye lidded.
Fingers touched to thumb.

Only look. What you hear
can tell you. But you
see your own way.

Bare Hands

Just that, nothing more, no internet,
facebook, mobile, knitting needles,
rolling pin, sledgehammer, hopes.

Just her silent palms face upward, ask,
what will I teach my children
now the world's new again,

speaks different languages,
talks to each other,
knows when liars or the confused

try to set the path? Just feel.
Just that she mustn't spoil.

There Ought To Be A Song 1

There ought to be a song about poets
who listen for silence then try to write it

interrupted by things which make them angry
or afraid – afraid's the hardest to admit.

About paper, pencils and books, the only places
where a day can park itself,

not get in anyone's way, be jostled,
break anything, be broken.

But who would try it, where would it get read?

Builders

It's noisier than you'd have liked
until they stop for lunch at an upturned crate,

their backs round, fingers clawed on sandwiches,
elbows on knees, heads cocked on phones,

they gaze, after they slug from a can or bottle,
wait for digestion, breath the silence.

Lunch doesn't talk much, it laughs.
Today's weather's a relief, cleaner.

Then they spring up to work, grit, noise,
heat their muscles, shut your mind.

First Generation

Poles renovate London; swing picks
and hammers, tense strong backs,

pivot at the knee, sink their heads,
pray at their tasks.

When this newest workforce goes
will the houses they build back home

replace the being there, that's in the children
they'd sent, dainty, to our schools, libraries,

gyms, the ones they'd bought computers for?
A lot stays behind in bricks and mortar,

and calloused hands embarrass
the families they try to build futures for.

Oil Slick

Swim in the deep sea, black,
stung with salt, shoaled fresh
with dolphin.

Fish off a ketch, cast a line
terrified you'll feel a pull,
need to reel something in.

Watch the night from an aft deck,
wish you'd eaten and drunk less,
as waves rise inside you.

Ignore the crushed onyx
that powders the feathers of birds,
silts the gills of fish you never see,

it stays on the television
for other people to disperse or hide.

Road Mender

Tonight he'll go out in the cold
in orange overalls and thermals
and lay matching cones
on the motorway.

Drivers will curse him
as he holds them up,
he'll be spot-lit by a friend
with stronger tungsten bulbs
than you get at a football field.

He'll man a pneumatic drill
and someone will say
from a crawling car,
they dug up that bit last week/
month/year, the bastards.

All this while his face freezes off,
his dinner's digested, and he's hungry again.

Magic Carpet

A whole family worked on this Qum's knots,
children's fingers are the most flexible,

they earn our bread. You'll take them to school,
we'll lose them and machines will do the work.

In halls of state, museums, palaces, you'll walk
on branches and curlicues, borders and spirals,

without understanding the language that hypnotises you
into a trance, takes you away from your own thoughts.

What will you teach our children in exchange?
With their pink fingers will they love any more?

And how will they remember what our food was like
after the hunger of a day's work?

Will they be served in their old age? Will anyone learn
what's needed for this hardest of jobs – know

they've earned it? Accept the time to travel with them
into the fantasies they want to imagine?

'She Wants To Land The Balloon'

She wants to land the balloon,
open it up and see what's inside.

Understand being carried on the breeze,
or in a cloud unknowing.

Unformed ideas are a destination,
a prayer when insight fails,
or rage impinges.

She wants to write a single quiet line
split by its own prism.

Old Recipes

Throw out ideas, books.
Work, exercise,

launder, clean,
make jam, cook cordon bleu

from the cheapest ingredients,
make dresses, do the garden,
don't be distracted by opinions.

That Kind Of War

That Kind Of War

Conscript us for that kind of war,
train us in manoeuvres
that cause women to be heard.

The infantry men of our generation
are tired from the efforts they've made
to support us.

We're still too quiet/loud/bold/
fearful. Give us weapons with truer aim.

Teach us how to use them.
We'll change our clothes, hair,
food, learn the languages

of the women who aren't free, the ones who are
and of those who will never be.

The Poetry Of Propaganda

The sound of truth dying,
death made holy,
women and children's lives
being traded in tear bottles.
The factioned blood of the terrified,
who aren't invited to contribute,
their job is to be afraid,
quiet except for that.
They've been a long time trained,
their reflexes honed
while they slept
lullabied by slogans, histories,
promises, threats.
Transported away from themselves,
they've learned to call their shadows
enemy, to stand away from them.
First to let other people kick them senseless,
then to watch the terrified, use carvers,
parers, nail-scissors, nappy-pins
to open veins.
Then there are those among them
who bring out food, humanity, they are also guilty.

War Poem

There are no heroic deaths in war,
round people up, they cry like stuck pigs,
run with a bayonet, you wet your pants,
kill with a drone, computer games
make you crazy when your kids play them.

For evil not to triumph good people
need do nothing but advocate, negotiate, react,
be diplomatic, watchful, mindful.

They need to listen, hear,
answer not placate, resist not fight,
determine not dominate, be dutiful not expectant.
And ramparts will give way to buttresses,
wars will be averted before
they grow tired, seed poppies,
make mounds, cinders of macheted limbs,
empty boy's bowels, girl's wombs.

Shooting Into The Corner

Visitors to the Royal Academy
laugh at "Shooting Into The Corner".
A pale soldier loads
a red paint projectile
into a canon three times an hour.

He embodies every new recruit,
clean, mechanical.

Looks through you.
He hasn't seen war,
can't watch its audiences
while he acts his part
in the orgy.

Akyn

The blind akyn who arrived
to sing solosinnya before death,
became chaff to be mulched and limed invisible.
The kobza, basolya, lira,
sopilka, trembita, drymba, trembled
sinewed songs as the volynka wheezed melodies.

They all came to Stalin's
"Life is Better, Life is Merrier" conference.
Believed what they heard,
in their unmapped villages.

Gathered the dispersed,
with their poems, music, history
and they were shot.

Stalin couldn't send revisions to blind men,
make authorised versions
of their minstrelled histories.

The time it would have taken to explain
to each akyn what was expected,
would have been too long.
This is their song.

Barrels

To wash a wine barrel we used to put a heavy chain inside,
hanging on a bar, fill it with cold water, from the well,
vines root deep, they don't need much water.
We'd close it up and rock so the chain knocked the inside.
For a while the water we let out looked like wine,
sediment I suppose. Then we'd refill and start again
until all the water ran clear. It was a hard job,
all the farming work was hard. We pruned in autumn,
used the cuttings for kindling, my Parisian hands
became like leather.

Gurs

The gendarmes ran Gurs,
thousands of us lay on the earth,
in corrugated iron huts, open at both ends.

Food, water and excrement came and went
in the same buckets, and at 3 in the morning
cattle-trucks rattled

when their diesel engines were started,
and their lights were trained on one another,
there was no electricity.

Sleeping teenagers were dragged out
into the freezing night, loaded up,
then taken to the railway station.

I knew if we left France for the labour camps
we'd never return. I told the Chef des Gendarmes
we were British from Boukhara, and we were to sent to Pau,

then taken to Paris by train, and held at St Denis
as Prisoners of War. Our papers saved us.

Welcome To Britain

My father came here hooked to the side
of a Douglas Dakota after Paris was liberated
and he left the prison camp at St Denis.
He came to do war work or volunteer.
We were British from Boukhara
for generations, we had huge white documents
which said so. We'd traded with the cottonopolis
of Manchester when the American fields
burned during the civil war, we'd interceded
with the Emir for the lives of Connolly and Stoddart
who'd been consigned to his snake pits.
But we were strangers when we came
to where I'd be born, go to grammar school,
find language, literatures, history, geographies,
to add to my own.

There Ought To Be A Song 2

For that poet, he sees so much
in his father. I hope the song
says that they spoke, hugged, ate,
laughed, that there was time
and scope for this love received
and given to be all it could.
There ought to be a song, dance,
smell, touch, sight unending.
And nothing left unexpressed
between them.

Avsonia

You know about coming from a country
that doesn't exist. About the belief
that if you were there it would.

That your grandparents and theirs held on,
afraid to shed blood, being afraid
of the blood they'd seen.

You know about coming from a country
which uses language to change the way you think,
to disenfranchise, or teach you to disenfranchise.

Which takes you into its schools, and gives you
every inch of the world that can be pasted
in a book but leaves your family out of things.

You don't want to be taught what a Jew is,
or what Israel can and can't be,
or what a Moslem is, needs, and how to respect her.

You speak her languages, eat her food, were her neighbour,
know how neighbours behave, and their husbands,
sons, fathers, brothers, uncles, and all their forebears.

Think Of Her

Think Of Her

Where mothers sit with children
at school gates. In dead-eyed parks,
in every chance there is to reclaim status,
in the still of before her body changed
or the search for what hasn't happened.
Think of her near every abandoned woman
who ends her marriage because her husband won't.
Think of her when a girl reads a book
with a boy-hero that every boy likes,
only girls like girl-heroes. Think of her
whenever you are a Jew,
ask what that means, ask why
you feel hurt from outside, inside.
When you study gemarra, think of her,
when you're illiterate, deaf, confused,
segregated, uncomprehending,
when you escape to a line of jumping prose,
a column of irreconcilable figures,
when you've got to drive children to a birthday party
and you turn left instead of right,
can't choose a present, face the parents
without losing your train of thought.
Think of her thinking, when you read poems
with lengthened, measured, halted, staggered breath;
from cities, suburbs, families, drawing rooms, breakdowns,
battle fields, when you get angry or soothed,
think of her finding love between poets who wouldn't cede
to the silence of death. Think of her cajoled, over sausages,
to publish translated visions, imagined transitions,
from four alphabets. Think of her going to sleep,
staying asleep, lying prone, hopeless

not fighting back until her grey hair and resolve measured
against that of others who had, did, would choose life
over living death, think of her when you fight knowledge,
endure grief you've made no way for.

'Keep Your Hands Busy'

Keep your hands busy,
your mind needs time
to cool your heart.

Ask a long list of questions,
answer none,
but understand that they exist.

Don't dare judge or pour yourself
into the chalice you're offered.
Don't drink or pass it on.

It's Good To Love

And marry a man of regular habits,
a kind man. To have children, teach them
to live by ancient rhythms, to question
as they live in a different present,
use old languages alongside the new.

It's good to have your own realm
near the one you came from,
to build vision which splits light,
makes surfaces on which
all that's left of tears are tides of salt.

The Mothers

The mothers go forth and multiply
although they're not commanded.
The mothers' bodies are invaded,
overtaken, always remember.
Their sleep's never the same again.

The mothers who woke before dawn to light fires,
still hear the central heating clank as they plan
for their households and their parents'. Remember
their grandparents, what they expected.

The mothers who gave birth to worry
or those without children who can't sleep
for the lack. Who feminise the fathers
then say they aren't men.

The mothers valued beyond rubies,
red with blood, bloodless, lustre haired,
or grey. The mothers lithe or lazy, artistic,
or who work for wages as they watch

mothers, who were their daughters,
or who are their son's wives.
The mothers obsolete now wisdom's asleep,
and generations aren't valued. The mothers
who won't make a treadmill of the new religion.

The Pram In The Hall

The carriage-built white Silver Cross
gathers dust on its taut navy rain-cover and huge hood,
reminds you of Milton, Pampers and Dreft.

Better sprung than the car,
too small once a baby gets to five months,
too big for the hall.

Reminds you of playgroups, schools, university,
weddings, grandchildren, divorces. Better than a picture,
sharper than a mirror, breaks your heart.

Earrings

Assayed and marked, the silver earrings
wait in their box for her to arrive.
She's sixteen and youth's giving her trouble.
You envy it but not its price.
Nothing you do now
will help the rift, but one day
as she fingers this gift, she'll think differently
about your efforts and why they stopped.

Lesson

You taught her to sing like a starfish,
arms and legs outstretched. To rock
from foot to foot, her flat hips stiff.
Both of you had the same profile,
your childhood was in the X of her body.

Then you lay her on the floor,
put a fat book on her abdomen,
talked to her straight legs, whispered,
that's it, as she exhaled a sound,

and you reminded her that babies breathe
from the diaphragm. Then the, *la,* you'd sung
came out of her. *You see, never say, "I can't,"*
you shouted, as you stood her up,
and put her palms on your ribs.
Then you both sang, soprano.

Concert

Interrogate the cello, become impatient with its strings,
your finger tips, the tuning pegs, stool height, but not her.

Today you're young enough to want this audience,
although you could be out on the streets busking,

The tramp's ukele was great, he played it like -
then I had a rap battle with him and two other bros -

You crease your eye edges, make dimples, show teeth when she
says,
Not Camden, that's all drugs –

make pouches on your cheek bones, lid your eyes,
stretch your neck, strum, pound rhythm with the base of your
thumb,
make her believe there's no danger.

Guests

Travel safe old parents without the need for oxygen,
without sore guts, bad circulation, nightmares,
fears of ayin hara.

Travel safe Apa whose ankles have thickened,
Khwar, who's as modern as aerobics.
Bring your fanciest clothes, trinkets,

gifts, brachot, goodies, stories for the henna.
Dances to heat the blood. Bring music and laughter
for me to pile on the bride and water for me to wash her in,

we have no use for the soil on your shoes,
wipe your feet before you leave Israel,
the earth will find us at the right time,
God spare us all for this day.

The Urge To Walk

Pre-senile and prone to going AWOL,
alternatives are proposed to you,
treadmill and television -
the mind can wander,
reclining bike -
no need for balance.

The words to explain, even to yourself,
the feel of gravel, grass, mud,
sound of traffic, rain, silence.
The first of freedoms, real, uncosted.
The first of somewhere to be.
And yes a dangerous end, with pain.

You won't be able to understand,
you will be a risk to others.
Dilemmas walk with you. Don't speak,
it explains a lot, if only for a moment.

Year

Wait before you disappear,
live without a reckoning,
before you eat the days,
drink the seasons.

I've got questions
I haven't even asked,
which are older than me.
Go slow so I can remember them

before white, green, yellow, turn to gold,
dust waits, shivers,
the exhausted earth gapes.
Rather let every day be endless
like Summer used to be.

Honoured

A Waiting Room

Made of nothing to rush for,
this place watches her breath
as she watches herself. She doesn't use
her eyes, because colours, shapes,
light have become peripheral.
Her mind's eye sees her rib cage
expand, her diaphragm settle, her nostrils
warm then cool. There's something
about a waiting room which makes her
forget, ignore, set aside, what she needs,
wants, has to do, there's something
that happens unsummoned.

How Did They Choose?

How did they choose?
Looks, brains, kindness, chemistry?
Their relatives liked each other,
the match was a success,
neither novelists nor poets
would ever write about it.

How To Beat Your Wife

If the husband wants to use beatings to treat his wife,
Yehjib, yehjib, yehjib
Allah yakuna al mama lahab.
Never, never, never, do it in front of the children.
It must remain between him and her.
The husband must not cause her to bleed.
The husband must not break any bones.
He should avoid her face and other
sensitive parts of her body.
If a person violates these rules
he violates the rules of Allah.
He cannot do whatever he wants with his wife
because she is not his merchandise.
Even if the wife forgives her husband
it doesn't mean Allah will on judgement day
So spoke Sheik Abdullah aal Mukhmoud
for Bahraini State TV on 20th June 2005.

Munir

(For Wafa Sultan)

You cry and say when you were little
your mother jumped on your feet
and pinched your clitoris when you were naughty,
say, *women imprison women.*

You tell me that you're ten. In fifteen years
you'll burn yourself to death, leave five children.
Today's your wedding day,
the groom's your uncle, he's fifty.

Pleureuse

She hit her forehead,
ululated,
then her eyes made her face wet,
her nose ran.

A low sound grew from her throat
into a shocking wail,
which made everyone cry
in their own key, all together.

Dina

Genesis 34

Shechem, son of Hamor the Hivite, raped me.
Then Hamor asked my father, Jacob, if Shechem
and I could marry, if all the Hivite men

could have Canaanite wives in return for gifts
and rights of settlement in their land.
My brothers told the Hivites,

if they were circumcised they could marry us.
As they recovered, my brothers killed them,
in their beds.

My voice is never heard,
what happened to me next
was never written.

Hannah and Elkanah
Samuel 1

Childless, but bounded by faith
I wait until thirst cries
in my nights, my empty arms.

Starve, though my table's full of food.
Then Elkanah hears a drunken voice
in my promise and says, *remember*.

Labour

Left her as empty as a baby
sucking air,
and high, her legs weak.
Raw, glad of pain,
as strong as her mother's
who she wanted to show
the daughter she was empty of,
now she couldn't have children.
She'd come to abort this baby
so she could marry,
start a family, at the right time.
The fever had gone on too long,
she was pregnant like a cantaloupe,
before he'd brought her here.
They'd come after dark,
the hospital had said, *we've saved you*,
but her womb was gone, and he was gone.
The social worker was there,
what use did she have for the social?
Better she'd have died.
Even if she explained to her family
how the birth control she'd wanted,
the medicine she'd begged for,
would've saved her,
even if they didn't kill her,
she'd still cry, *please save the baby*.

Honoured

Ach yarab, she says as she hits
her head with rubble. *Ach yarab,*
she wails, as she slaps her cheeks.
As her husband covers her she feels nothing
because she's been bitten away
by her grandmother. *Ach yarab,* she cries,
as she gives birth to the shahida.
Ach yarab, she says as she feeds her
with ecstasy and closes away from the mundane.
Ach yarab, as she lays iron on her girls and honey
on her boys. *Ach yarab,* when her husband hits her,
when her mother jumps on her feet,
when the glance of her mother-in-law
calls in the cut which kills her.

In a Hotel Lobby

The soldier and the pilot
wait for their luggage.
She smiles the evidence of their night,
he stands behind her, straight backed,
relaxed, at home.
Her joy's an aura,
his, a proximity.

Advice

You say learn my language,
forget your own,
it brings new ideas, possibilities,
gives you an alphabet you never had
as your mother whispered secrets
she'd learned from hers,
which she never understood.
It can spell those secrets,
define them for you, then we can move on.
Your mother's dead or never born,
there are different ways to know,
ways she never dreamed,
possibilities not whispered, hinted at,
unnameable.
Because everything's a part of speech
and everything's translatable.
The page, screen, word, deed, enunciated
is progress.
There're no questions you can't answer, re-answer,
change your mind about
if you listen, fine tune, use my cadences,
don't be afraid, you won't lose yourself.

Jews

Sabena Spielrein

Your daughters Eva and Renata,
were shot at your side,
but your names weren't wiped from the record.

The freedom you'd learned and could teach
merely by your presence, footfall, empathy,
came from illness understood, surmounted.

Confused child, precluded professional, Jewess,
mother-midwife-of-death wasn't what you'd planned,
but when you hid your diary under the siddur-rest

in that Rostov shul, you railed against a void,
internal, external, eternal, for your good life,
and for the girlhoods you'd made so different to yours.

Korczak

The trees at Ein Harod waited for your children
to climb them. You noticed the absence of squirrels
and wondered if the British Consul would send some
as an advance party.

They'd taken their time when you'd written
to ask for napkins but once they'd replied,
they'd sent enough for generations to come.

Your children's hands were the cleanest in Poland.
Oh Poland, with hindsight could you have left sooner,
to where Ashkenazim would sun-burn and Sephardim
meet the cousins they'd left behind,

to where history would live on in cooking pots,
and children from old countries would meet on new websites,
talk, sing, laugh, eat fast, pray slow, cross continents.

1956

Those men don't travel well,
the women with their recipes, gossip,
jokes, *sakhtet bent*, bring Egypt with them.

But youth drains out of engineers. And Fayed's merchants,
who miss drinking with their English business partners
after work at Groppi, never get used to it here.

They dream of sharkskin suits, horse-drawn traps,
Alexandria's criosette, the Cure at Helwan,
nights in Heliopolis; their families can't revive them
with, *raconte un peu*. They fade without sunlight.

Mishkenot Sha'ananim: Yemin Moshe
(In memory of Yehuda Amichai)

1. Red Roofs

They slant on to Jerusalem stone walls,
which pour down the hillside
then stop, neat, obedient above the Sultan's pool.
This whole quarter's obedient,
stands to attention, clean
well-dressed, its creepers trimmed
closer than when artists lived here,
or when the first residents went back
to sleep inside the city's walls at night,
because they felt safer.

2. Aqua Blue Railings

Compete bravely with the Lebanese cedars
on the hillside across the way,
to pierce the evening sky with their sharp finials.
Churchill's bust greens in sympathy
with the olive trees.
Some French visitors chat
in the same tone as the last birds sing,
introduce geography to a place
which stands outside it.

Gilad Shalit

I'm not a hostage to fortune,
or a whipping boy.
I'm a quiet chalice
replete with hope,

I'll walk up the stairs
of Shiffa hospital's basement,
across the stones of Tallel Howa
and the green plains of Zeitun
towards Raffah.

Thousands of men and women
will walk towards me.
I and they will see
only our mothers. Our fathers
will take us inside tents
open on four sides, will wash
our feet, our hands, feed us
and then we'll be given
ploughshares.

Jews

(In Memory of Czesław Miłosz)

We're neither poems for you to fetishise
nor emblems of the murdered of the twentieth century,
we don't hold all possibilities in our Talmudic minds
live burdened with the grief you want us to.
We're not the monsters of the Middle East,
the devils of the diaspora, nor do we know
the selves we recognise in one another.
We're in danger in your midst
and where you don't know us,
a barometer of your pasts and futures
that you never consult,
and yet we ourselves live
by the tremble of mercury
which we always ask ourselves to shape,
for which we're quoted against ourselves.
There's no monopoly of suffering
what did the first victims know
who's parents sent them with wobbly legs,
gaped mouths, vacant grins, rage, the evidence
of the trial they were to heart, hands, purse;
yes, look I'm a Jew and I've said purse,
judge me if you want; the first victims
were piped away like Hamlyn's children,
only before the rats and other vermin.

Arab Spring

Her enemy wears a cruel flag
which used to frighten her until his cause imploded.
Among power seekers and self-enrichers sprang idealists,
with great plans, some of which could have changed
a generation and history beyond. She and her friends
protested too, about cottage cheese, food's expensive,
woman cannot live on Hi Tech and Start Ups alone.
So she wore what her enemy wore and they both spoke out
and were ignored.

She knows she's got it better.
In Israel roads are paved, hospitals clean, so relaxed
the beds roll out onto terraces and patients, doctors, nurses,
relatives, smoke side-by-side in the sun. Races and religions,
care and are cared for interchangeably. Look the borders
are complicated for everyone, walls, iron domes,
young people's best years, old people's failures,
incontrovertible hate in her enemies' textbooks,
the world's obsession.

Gut your own fish, shell your peas
tarmac your roads, ring your Church bells,
tweet, text, facetime/book, BBM,
lap top, tablet, think, but be less shrill,
she's trying to listen, watch, see the difference
between her enemy's wife and her. Her child,
his, her grandchild, his, her mother, and his.

In her father she recognises the victim-cynic,
shrewd survivor's, *be careful*,
be observant her faith teaches her,
with a lot a helpful rules. Her mother's
training, tastes, pangs, rigour are inescapable,

go on like a private joy.
Can a woman's enemy stop her feeling?
Her child overwhelm her?
Are our mirrors un-silvered windows?
Can we touch each other
against them, each on our own side?

Syria

Can you hear anything, you whose roofs
are dangerous? Is there anything she can say
to you? It's not her turn. She understands,
politics makes opponents, but you shouldn't die.
Now its burning skin and Sunnis, Shias, Kurds,
Christians, Alawites, crushed like Coke cans
which make junk of your roads, villages.
Not everywhere fights you know,
refugees are ignored somehow
in every war zone,
people transcend, wait it out
with someone else's household
between them and the front line.
There are those who bear witness afterwards,
deny, never see. How does that work?
The ones who sand the shul floor in Curaçao,
the Childits, the Italians, handsome
in their uniforms at Groppi, the Raj mourned,
St. Denis sentimentalised or favoured after Gurs,
as though ranking were a reflex of survival.

Seder

And there it is among the leftovers,
table-planned, fed, clothed, sung, travelled,
tasted, salt-watered, bitter-herbed, haroséted, gemarahéd;
where you cut your egg (only mourners eat an egg whole),
where you want to mourn, swallow embers
that dry in your mouth,
forget the six million, their gentile relatives
in the family of murder, spit out bitterness,
which makes you afraid, stop the ones
that did it, those you can reach, go back, kill
that time in childhood when you understood,
not without parents, just camps, Suez.
It's easier to be a child now,
new starts are endless.
Why do you tremble, why does your tongue burn?

The Hendonists
(After Sean O'Brien's 'Novembrists')

It's got to be written of us that we were happy,
some in Brampton, some in Alexandra Road,

some with Kosher Kingdom sushi, some fed by Gift,
others still cooking their own kugel/hamim.

It's got to be written that all the different shuls
made a back-and-forth, that shirs furrowed brows,

that women hugged big Talmuds, men tucked them under-arm
and both stood foot-to-foot, outside, waiting for lifts for 5 minute drives.

It's got to be written that the bell never stopped ringing after 9
and some never gave at the door, others always did,

parents, children, housekeepers handed reluctant
embarrassed, generous or indifferent pennies, pounds,

fivers to charismatic or coarse shnorers,
whose drivers' engines idled as they checked their lists.

Business, duty – this small sector
of the mechanics of self help?

They've got to be named: Norwood/Ravenswood, Jewish Care,
Emunah, Wizo, Harif, Kisharon, Camp Simcha. The school boards:

Hasmo, Yavneh, the Independent, Sinai, Mathilda-Marks, Yesohday-'a-Tora;
their graduates' destinations: yeshiva, sem, hakhshara, Jewniversity

shidduchs or makhal (un-analogous to ISISian brides or Syrian bullies),

jobs, marriage, births, pedions, brisses, simhat bats, b'mitzvahs,
bikur holims, shivas, Bushey, Waltham Abbey, Hoop Lane, Edgware.
Friday nights, shabbes lunches, seudas, hagim, shlakh-manot, saplings,

fancy dress, drunks, lulavs, succahs, apples, honey, Alex Shajer's bee hives,
fasts, feasts, flowers. Our hakafohted, cleaned, khallah baked, b'dikatid, bathed,

de-hametzed, memounah'd kaleidescope must be looked into
before its twisted, turned, worded, why'd, worried over.

It's got to be written that we were happy day by day; embedded,
layered, accustomed, institutioned, libraried, shabbes-urned,

idiomed, grammared, minhag'd even, as we took the temperature
with our elbows, looked at, or were blind to, a future we were written out of.

Languaged

Languaged by conquerers
behind whom whisper ancients,
ahead, dominions.

On rainy streets, by rivers
silvered in August sun,
under London's eye, Burford's bridge,

by Bealey's village hall, Leeds' canal.
You read books for answers,
but say little.

Search the landscape
for nuance, or some of it,
but not in the way of being reflected,

by now you understand,
this isn't your condition,
something you have a choice about.

Glossary

Aramaic

Gemarah	p74	Talmud

Biblical Hebrew

ayin hara	p46	The evil eye.
brachot	p46	Blessings.
Haroset	p74	Paste made of cinnamon, sweet wine and chopped nuts, a symbol of the mortar used by Jewish slaves in Ancient Egypt.
Seder	p74	Rituals before the Passover meal, literally Order [of service]

Egyptian Arabic

Ach yarab	p59	Onomatopoeic word for a sigh.
Sakhtet bent	p67	Contraction of "as quiet as the house on the day a girl's born"
Shahida:	p59	Female martyr

French

Pleureuse	p55	Professional wailer. Often employed at Eastern funerals.
Raconte un peu	p67	Tell us a story

Judaio Tajik

Apa	p46	Older sister.
Khwar	p46	Younger sister.

Spanish

Brascenos	p11	Braziers

Notes

An End (p11)
Between 25,000 and 200,000 Spanish peasants are estimated
to have died of hunger from 1939 to 1953 while the country
was a net exporter of high calorie foods. In his biography, "Life
Without Armour" (Harper Collins, 1995), Alan Sillitoe describes
the method used by some parents to kill themselves, and their
starving families.

Shooting Into The Corner (p28)
A work by Anish Kapoor installed at the Royal Academy of Arts,
London, in 2009.

Akyn (p29)
Dmitri Shostakovich describes these murders in his memoir
"Testimony" co-written with Solomon Volkov, (Limelight
Editions 2004).

Barrels (p30)
Charles Mammon, the author's father farmed in St Porquet in
Vichy France during World War II, until the gendarmes deported
him to Gurs a concentration camp in the French Pyrenees.

Gurs (p31)
This account of Charles Mammon (1923-), pertains to
him and his brother Joseph (1924-2011). For the latter's
evidence to Stephen Spielberg see www.youtube.com/
watch?v=nMvlcagQkOg

Welcome To Britain (p32)
Colonels Stoddart and Connolly both died on the orders of the
Emir of Boukhara, who decided on 24th June 1842 that they
were British spies.

The Mothers (p41)
Jews apply the Biblical commandment peru oo revoo (go forth and multiply) only to men, since women's lives can be threatened by giving birth and the sanctity of life is held paramount.

Guests (p46)
soil on your shoe – It is an age old Jewish custom to bury the dead with a small amount of soil from the holy land.

Sabena Spielrein (p65)
Sabena Spielrien (1855-1942). A pioneering female psychoanalyist, student and colleague of Carl Gustav Jung.

Korczak (p66)
Janusz Korczak aka Dr Henryk Goldszmit (1878 1942), Polish-Jewish children's author, educator and paediatrician who gave up private practice to run an enlightened childrens' home and died in Treblinka with his charges.
Ein Harod, kibbutz where, in 1934, Korczak visited a former colleague to examine conditions and teaching methods.

1956 (p67)
After the 1956 Suez Crisis Egypt's Jews were expelled in the main.

Lightning Source UK Ltd.
Milton Keynes UK
UKHW040746281118
333066UK00001B/51/P